One-Minute Promises of Comfort

STEVE MILLER

HARVEST HOUSE PUBLISHERS

EUGENE, OREGON

Cover by Terry Dugan Design, Minneapolis, Minnesota

Cover photo © Photodisc / Photodisc Blue / Getty Images

ONE-MINUTE PROMISES OF COMFORT
Copyright © 2007 by Steve Miller
Published by Harvest House Publishers
Eugene, Oregon 97402

ISBN-13: 978-0-7369-1943-2
ISBN-10: 0-7369-1943-0

Printed in the United States of America

07 08 09 10 11 12 13 / BP-CF / 10 9 8 7 6 5 4 3 2 1

Our light affliction,
which is but for a moment,
is working for us a far more
exceeding and eternal weight of glory.

2 Corinthians 4:17

With wholehearted gratitude to God
for His unceasing faithfulness.
Through each trial I experience,
I have come to see more and more
of His greatness.

Contents

For Those Who Hurt

∽

Suffering has a way of bringing both confusion and clarity to our lives. It is in the cold winter storms of affliction that we become disoriented, unsure of what to do or where to go. Our hearts ache for the warm rays of God's comfort and assurance, and we struggle with the deeper questions of life: *Why me? What did I do to deserve this? Why hasn't God answered my cry for help?*

As we become focused on our pain, all else becomes insignificant by comparison. Suddenly the everyday pursuits of life lose their attraction. We realize the treasures of this world are meaningless and unfulfilling. We now long for the simplest things—peace, joy, and rest. That is, the things only God can give us.

Affliction drives us into the waiting arms of our heavenly Father like nothing else does. Desperate to escape the howling winds around us, we seek shelter with Him. It is at times like this we are most willing to listen to Him, most ready to hear what He has to say.

You'll find His tender words of encouragement all through this book—words of love, of compassion, and of comfort. These words appear in the form of promises you can cling to in your moments of difficulty.

Read on, and get to know the promises from the One who is called the God of All Comfort. And let Him renew you, lift you up, and fill you with hope.

Help When You Are Helpless

When God lays men on their backs,
then they look up to heaven.

THOMAS WATSON

The Ultimate Helper

*I will lift up my eyes to the hills—from whence
comes my help? My help comes from the LORD,
who made heaven and earth.*

PSALM 121:1-2

Where do you look when you need help? Is your
first instinct to look up to your heavenly Father…and
to *continue* looking to Him all through your difficult
circumstance?

When problems come our way, they usually come
with the temptation to resolve them through human
strength rather than divine. Or if God doesn't help us
quickly enough or in the way we want Him to, we question
Him. Or we give up and sink into despair.

Yet God truly is our only hope. There is no one more
powerful than Him. No one more efficient. No one more wise.
No one more faithful. No one more loving. No one can
outdo God when it comes to help.

And His help is never too little or too late. We may
not understand His ways or His timing. But we *can* trust
Him who made heaven and earth. He who *made* all can
do all.

Look to Him alone, and help will come.

Counting on Him

I will strengthen you, yes, I will help you.

Isaiah 41:20

How will I ever get through this?

That's the question we often ask ourselves when faced with a trial that overwhelms us. We become discouraged to the point of resignation or despondency. We feel like giving up because we are unable to see any glimmer of hope.

From our earthly perspective, a problem may look like Mount Everest. But from God's heavenly perspective, it's not even a grain of sand. There is no difficulty that can challenge His strength. He is the omnipotent One, the all-powerful One. And He promises, "I will strengthen you, yes, I will help you."

That which exhausts you to nothingness is nothing to God. When you wait and lean upon Him, He will give you unexpected strength. He who has proven Himself by helping you in the past will not cease to help you in the future. God didn't say, "I *might* help you." He said, "I *will*."

Yes, you can count on Him.

Nothing Too Hard for God

Behold, I am the LORD, the God of all flesh. Is there anything too hard for Me?

JEREMIAH 32:27

If God can help the most wretched of sufferers, then He can help us.

In the Bible, a supreme example of one who suffered is Job. In one day, he lost all his livestock, most of his servants, and all his children. Then he was afflicted with terrible sores all over his body. And instead of gaining sympathy from his wife and friends, he received harsh criticism. Yet with God's help, Job persevered, and was blessed abundantly in the end.

The apostle Paul also suffered greatly: "Five times I received forty stripes minus one. Three times I was beaten with rods; once I was stoned; three times I was shipwrecked; a night and a day I have been in the deep…in weariness and toil, in sleeplessness often, in hunger and thirst, in fastings often, in cold and nakedness" (2 Corinthians 11:24-25,27).

It was with God's help that Job and Paul were able to endure such severe trials, and it is with God's help that we can do the same. Our God is a mighty God, and no trial is too great for Him to handle.

The Certainty of Deliverance

He will deliver the needy when he cries, the poor also, and him who has no helper.

PSALM 72:12

When you have no other resource, no other helper, when all else has failed, you can depend wholly upon God. His help is not just a possibility, but an absolute certainty.

Frequently when problems arise, we try to handle them on our own at first. With determination we try to extinguish a small blaze, only to see it turn into a horrific inferno. Why don't we go to our heavenly Father in the first place? Won't His help always be the best we can get? Isn't there wisdom in seeking the One who has already planned our days, and who alone knows exactly what we need today so we are ready for tomorrow?

When we run to God with our plea, let's set aside any expectations about how deliverance will come. God's plans are often different than ours, but they are always better.

You who are needy, go to Him who has everything. You who are poor, go to Him who is rich. You who have no helper, seek Him who is more than able!

14

Help in the Day of Trouble

Call upon Me in the day of trouble; I will deliver you, and you shall glorify Me.

PSALM 50:15

In our moments of despair, Satan wants very much to convince us there is no hope and that God has surely forgotten us. He wants to drive the wedge of doubt between us and God so we might stop seeking, stop believing, and stop trusting.

Yet in Psalm 50:15, God *commands* us to cry out to Him for help. His deliverance may not come immediately, but it will come. And note that God does not say, "I *might* deliver you," but rather, "I *will* deliver you."

Scripture affirms again and again that God keeps His promises. If you are His child, then this promise applies to you too. It is a promise you can cling to without fear of disappointment, an anchor you can hold firm to no matter how rough the seas of life become.

God does not lack the power to help you. Call upon Him, and He will save you. And when He does, remember to thank and glorify Him.

Resting in His Faithfulness

Far above all finite comprehension is the unchanging faithfulness of God. Everything about God is great, vast, incomparable. He never forgets, never fails, never falters, never forfeits His word.

A.W. PINK

Fear Not!

*Fear not, for I am with you; be not dismayed, for
I am your God. Yes, I will help you, I will uphold
you with My righteous right hand.*

ISAIAH 41:10

Fear of the unknown…of failure…of pain…of loss.
Whatever the reason, fear often leaves you feeling weak
and helpless. Here, your heavenly Father lovingly calls
your attention to four great truths for those times when
fear seizes your heart:

I am with you. Fear has a way of making you feel all
alone. But you have God's assurance He is with you. He
is at your side.

I am your God. Your companion is no less than God
Himself! There is no greater resource you could ask for
in your time of need.

I will help you. You're not on your own. You don't
have to figure out the solution yourself. God will enable
you to carry on.

I will uphold you. The very hand that upholds the
entire universe is the same hand that upholds you.

You may be weak, but you will not fall. God is strong
and faithful. Fear not!

A Shelter in the Storms

*God is our refuge and strength, a very present help
in trouble. Therefore we will not fear, even though
the earth be removed, and though the mountains be
carried into the midst of the sea.*

PSALM 46:1-2

There is absolutely nothing in this world that can give
us true security from life's calamities. No one is immune
to heartbreak, disease, or disaster. No one can make it all
the way through life without experiencing disappointment,
hurt, or loss.

Though we cannot avoid the storms that come our
way, we can choose to seek shelter in the midst of them.
God is a mighty fortress in which we can seek protection
from even the worst of tribulations. Even when mountains
fall and the earth is shaken, God is not shaken. He is a
firm foundation on which we can stand, a strong shield
behind which we can hide.

That is why we can say with the psalmist, "Therefore
we will not fear." Yes, we will suffer, but we do not need
to be afraid. Though we may hurt, we can be filled with
comfort and infused with strength, for God is "a very
present help." He is right beside us, ready to assist us *every*
step of the way.

He Will Never Fail You

Who is mighty like you, O LORD? Your faithfulness also surrounds You.

PSALM 89:8

Because of our limited understanding and our inability to see from God's perspective, we will sometimes struggle with the thought that God has failed us. In such times we need to remind ourselves of some wonderful assurances found in Scripture:

God's mercies cannot cease. Because God is infinite, His mercies are infinite as well. They are new every morning (Lamentations 3:22-23). Every new day begins with a new supply of His goodness to us.

His presence cannot be removed. No matter where we go, God is with us. We could not hide from Him even if we wanted to (Psalm 139:7-10). Nothing can take us out of His hand (John 10:28-29).

His promise cannot fail. "There has not failed one word of all His good promise" (1 Kings 8:56). Because God is totally sovereign and all-powerful, nothing can keep Him from doing what He says He will do.

For these reasons, it is impossible for God to fail us. Though we can never be certain about life, we can always be certain about God. Great is His faithfulness!

An Anchor for Our Hearts

*You also be patient. Establish your hearts, for the
coming of the Lord is at hand.*

JAMES 5:8

When the way before us becomes dark, when we
search in vain for hope, where can we find consolation?
James 5:8 encourages us with these words:

Be patient. Don't grow weary; don't give up. Don't
think because an answer has not come that there *is* no
answer. God has promised to watch and preserve you. Be
patient, and let Him do what only He can do.

Establish your heart. When we fret, our minds and
hearts are tossed about by the winds of uncertainty.
We worry and speculate about that which has not yet
happened. Yet God beckons us to anchor our hearts in
Him. He alone is a sure foundation, an immovable rock,
an unshakable mountain.

For the coming of the Lord is at hand. We do not know
when He will return, but we do know that He *will* return.
And when He does, He will set all things right. All the
travails of life and the tears in our eyes will disappear.
And we will experience joy eternal—a joy we cannot even
imagine!

Always Watching

The eyes of the LORD are on the righteous, and His ears are open to their cry.

PSALM 34:15

At times, we may feel as though God is asleep when we cry out to Him. No matter how desperate or intense our cry, God does not seem to hear us. Why is that? In our search for answers, we can rule out the following:

> *God does not sleep.* "He who keeps you will not slumber" (Psalm 121:3).

> *God does not forget us.* "I will never leave you nor forsake you" (Hebrews 13:5).

> *God does not hide from us.* "I am with you always" (Matthew 28:20).

So what are we to do? Remember what is true about God—"the eyes of the LORD are on the righteous, and His ears are open to their cry." And notice that all through the psalms, those who cried out to God were persistent in their prayers, their pleas, and their pursuit. They never gave up.

God's eyes are on you at this very moment…and you can count on His faithfulness.

Are We Prepared?

Many are the afflictions of the righteous, but the
LORD delivers him out of them all.

PSALM 34:19

No matter what the affliction, we have the promise that God will deliver us "out of them all." In our suffering, we can have absolute, unreserved confidence God will do His part.

But what about our part? It is only right and wise for us to make God our refuge *before* trials come. Why wait until the storm is upon us before we take protective measures? The ready Christian will store up in his or her heart promises from Scripture that apply to the specific emergencies of life. God's promises are like buoyant lifeboats that keep us afloat when the violent seas of affliction threaten to plunge us into the dark depths of doubt.

The more diligent we are to pursue God and store up His promises in our hearts, the more we will be able to stay above our afflictions rather than be drowned by them. For then our hearts will be filled with hope instead of despair, and we will find ourselves able to sing, "God is our refuge and strength, a very present help in trouble. Therefore we will not fear" (Psalm 46:1-2).

His Unfailing Love

Ultimately the love of God is the basis for all our hopes. It is the object of our deepest longings. It is the source and fulfillment of our faith. It is the very basis for His grace to us. After all, we love Him only because He first loved us (1 John 4:19). And His love is also the guarantee of eternal bliss.

JOHN MACARTHUR

An Abiding Love

I have loved you with an everlasting love.

JEREMIAH 31:3

Trials have a way of making us feel as though God has forgotten us or cast us aside. And in the times when our difficulties continue on and on, we wonder if He hears our prayers anymore. "Haven't I already struggled long enough?" we cry. "When will this end?"

In the times when you wonder about God's love, remember Jeremiah 31:3. His love for you is everlasting. It will never change; it will never end.

God chose you to become His child in eternity past. And you will live and reign with Him in eternity future. He planned every day of your life in advance, and He has incredible blessings waiting for you in heaven. His love for you is so great He was willing to die for you. There's no greater love than that.

His love is an abiding love, an unshakable love, a forever love. Don't ever let doubt convince you otherwise.

Reminders of God's Love

*Will the Lord cast off forever? And will He be
favorable no more?...Has God forgotten to be
gracious? Has He in anger shut up His tender
mercies?...I will remember the works of the LORD;
surely I will remember Your wonders of old.*

PSALM 77:7-9,11

Trials are sweetened by the assurance of God's perfect
and unceasing love. When life gets difficult we may doubt
whether God really loves us, but we cannot argue with
the most magnificent display of love in all history—that
of God giving up His Son on the cross so that He might
gain us for all eternity.

When our hurts tempt us to question God, we need to
do as the psalmist did: We need to "remember the works of
the LORD," and His "wonders of old." Looking to the past
evidences of God's love can give us comfort and courage
for the future. And remembering His faithfulness to us
yesterday can stir our confidence for today.

God has not forgotten to be gracious to you. He loves
you, and He has your highest good in mind. When you
rest in the truth that your heavenly Father loves you with
a perfect and everlasting love that will never fade, you'll
find your heart filled with a peace that helps make your
trials more bearable.

The Greatness of God's Love

[Nothing] shall be able to separate us from the love of God which is in Christ Jesus our Lord.

ROMANS 8:39

Do you have any idea just how much God loves you?

Even though "we were still sinners, Christ died for us" (Romans 5:8). Even though "there is none who seeks after God" (Romans 3:11), God pursued us. Even though we "were by nature children of wrath" (Ephesians 2:3), God transformed us into children of light.

If God held nothing back when it came to our greatest need of all, will He hold anything back when it comes to our lesser needs? If He paid the ultimate sacrifice even when we didn't ask for it, how much more will He give good things to us when we do ask?

On the cross, God gave to us freely, not reluctantly. He gave His all, not just a portion. He gave a gift that lasts forever, not one that perishes with time.

Infinite love never changes. If life's problems have made you think otherwise, remember that God's love for you is constant. *Nothing* can change His love for you... ever!

The Love that Protects

The eyes of the Lord are on those who fear him, on those whose hope is in his unfailing love.

PSALM 33:18 NIV

Have you ever considered that God's watchfulness over you has probably saved you from potential dangers you didn't know about?

When we pray, we usually thank God for the things we have. But what about the things we *don't* have—things from which we have been spared? Perhaps our heavenly Father has guided our steps so as to help us avoid serious accidents or sickness. Or He has sheltered us from temptations that would have been too overwhelming to resist. Or He has prevented circumstances that would have brought grief or heartache too great for us to bear.

It is because the eyes of the Lord are upon you that life isn't more difficult than you are able to handle. He is always ready to intervene and redirect your steps, if necessary. So when it comes to walking the rough paths of life, it makes sense for you to place your hope in Him alone. He loves you with an unfailing love, and He will lead you safely home.

His Unceasing Goodness

*Nothing good comes except from God and
nothing except good comes from God.*

JOHN BLANCHARD

Surrounded by Mercy

*He who trusts in the L*ORD*, mercy shall surround him.*

PSALM 32:10

The person who puts his or her trust in God is surrounded by mercy—what a source of comfort and assurance in the midst of the trials and sorrows of life!

In mercy, our heavenly Father gives us what we do not deserve. He gives to us freely and generously—to the point of surrounding and protecting us completely. His mercy is all around us, though we may not see it.

Where is your trust? Are you trying to summon up strength from within? Have you placed your confidence in others around you? Or have you genuinely surrendered *all*—and nothing less than all—your hope to the Lord alone?

There's no reason to hold back. The reward God promises here is too great. To be surrounded on all sides by His mercy is to enjoy God's goodness at all times, in all places.

A Mercy That Never Ends

...who remembered us in our lowly state, for His mercy endures forever.

PSALM 136:23

Even when we are undeserving and forgetful, God remembers us. We are always in His thoughts and upon His heart. His concern and compassion are constant; nothing in our lives goes unnoticed by Him.

Imagine! He whose rule extends to every corner of the universe is thinking about you right now. We're not talking about a hairbreadth of attention that is fleeting because of the countless other demands that are upon Him. Because He is omnipresent and omnipotent, He is able to give His full attention to every one of His children at all times.

That God's mercy endures forever is evidence that He remembers us. Even in the midst of heartbreak, even when we are destitute, even when we just can't take it anymore, His mercy still shines warmly upon us—in the form of love, goodness, forgiveness, compassion, protection, and more. Even in life's unthankful moments, we have reason to be thankful.

God Never Makes Mistakes

*You are the God who does wonders; You have
declared Your strength among the peoples.*

PSALM 77:14

*Why is this happening to me, God? Surely there is some
mistake!*

That's probably what the Israelites were thinking
when, after they left slavery in Egypt, they had been unable
to find any water in the wilderness for three days. And
when they did find water, it was too bitter to drink. Then
the people complained of thirst. After all, without water,
they would die (Exodus 15:22-25).

It's important to note the people hadn't done anything
wrong. Nor had they strayed from God's directions. So
why did the Lord allow this? He had a purpose; He had
things He wanted to teach His people. And afterward,
consistent with His goodness, God did a wonderful work
and lead the Israelites to an oasis abounding with good
water (verse 27).

Are you in the wilderness now, kneeling before bitter
water? Perhaps you feel God has made a mistake. But God
never does. He has His purposes, and we need to trust
Him. And when His work is accomplished, He will lead
you to sweet water.[1]

He Will Never
Disappoint You

*The greatest sin of every Christian, and
the Christian church in general, is to limit
the eternal, absolute power of God to the
measure of our own minds and concepts
and understandings.*

MARTYN LLOYD-JONES

The Power of Trusting God

He will not be afraid of evil tidings; his heart is steadfast, trusting in the LORD.

PSALM 112:7

Because we live in a fallen world, bad things can and will happen. We never know, from moment to moment, when devastating news or circumstances may hit without warning. And then there are those situations in which we wait with dread, wondering whether the outcome will be favorable or take a turn for the worse.

Psalm 112:7 tells us that those who have placed all their trust in the Lord will remain steadfast when the bad news does come. It's when we rely completely on God that we will not find ourselves shaken. It's when we are fully confident in God's ability to sustain us that a change in our circumstances will not change our poise.

This strength to stand strong comes not from within us, but from our heavenly Father. It comes from our trust in what *He* can do, not what we can do.

Are you afraid? God is greater than the worst thing that could happen to you. Determine to trust Him, no matter what comes your way. Unwavering faith is the cure to unsettling fear.

God Only, God Alone

Truly my soul silently waits for God; from Him comes
my salvation. He only is my rock and my salvation;
He is my defense; I shall not be greatly moved.

PSALM 62:1

If only we would wait upon God alone in *all* things!
We say we trust Him, but within us the surrender is not
complete. We set one foot upon the solid rock of God's
might and the other foot upon the sinking sands of human
wisdom. And as the weight of our trials press down upon
us, given enough time, we slip and fall—all because we
didn't place our complete trust in God.

In the original Hebrew text of Psalm 62, the word
only or *alone* appears five times in the first eight verses.
And in every instance, *only* or *alone* is at the beginning of
the verse, clearly for emphasis. King David, the writer of
this psalm, was under attack by his enemies, and yet in
the face of that danger he knew absolute calm because his
confidence in God was complete.

As one writer said long ago, "They trust not God *at*
all who trust not him *alone*."[2] Have you given Him your
problem and let go of it? Are you willing to wait patiently
and expectantly, knowing that no one can protect you and
save you as He can?

Holding Fast onto God

Let us hold fast the confession of our hope without
wavering, for He who promised is faithful.

HEBREWS 10:23

"This is more than I can bear, Lord. Why won't you take away my pain?"

"What did I do to deserve this affliction?"

"Why is life so easy for the wicked and difficult for the Christian?"

When we ask questions like these, we need to stop and remember: We possess finite human minds that are trying to figure out the ways of an infinite God. There will come times when we cannot understand. Cannot find answers. Cannot make sense of it all.

This brings us to an important truth: What you think about God will influence how you respond to trials. If you believe that His wisdom and love are perfect and that He has your best interests in mind, the questions asked above won't rattle you. But if you have doubts about God, you'll have anxiety every step of the way through your trial.

The better you know God and His promises, the better you will respond when things go wrong. So hold fast. Don't waver, "for He who promised is faithful."

Replacing Fear with Trust

Be strong and of good courage, do not be afraid,
nor be dismayed, for the LORD your God is with
you wherever you go.

JOSHUA 1:9

Fear—whether imagined or real—can cause you to fall into the sin of doubting God. And when you doubt Him, you become worried and anxious. This, in turn, will rob you of your joy and peace.

When you are afraid of your circumstances, you can safely say you have not placed your confidence in God. Fear and trust cannot coexist at the same time in your heart. When confronted with fear, you need to make a deliberate choice and say you will "be strong and of good courage," and "not be afraid." Why? Because "God is with you wherever you go." With Him at your side, victory is assured.

Don't give fear a foothold in your heart. When you recognize it for what it is, surrender it immediately. And turn your thoughts to what God is capable of doing.

When you replace your fear with trust, you'll know the wonderful inner peace that comes from resting in God's care and strength.

The Beautiful Side
of Affliction

*Afflictions, they are but our Father's
goldsmiths who are working to
add pearls to our crowns.*

THOMAS BROOKS

God's Power in Us

Most gladly I will rather boast in my infirmities,
that the power of Christ may rest upon me.

2 CORINTHIANS 12:9

Affliction creates within us a deep feeling of want for God, for Christ, for heaven, for eternity. It is when we suffer that we come to realize how helpless we are and how hopeless our world is. Trials have a way of nudging us toward a more total dependence upon God, a more fervent embracing of Christ, and a more constant yielding to the Holy Spirit.

As life's difficulties compel us to draw closer to our heavenly Father, we become more and more a vessel through which He can do His work. One writer long ago said that "it is in answer to earnest longings, pantings, hungerings, and thirstings of the spirit that the Lord manifests Himself in the most remarkable manner."[3]

God Himself said, "My strength is made perfect in weakness" (2 Corinthians 12:9). It is when we are weakest that God's grace and power shines brightest. That is why the apostle Paul could conclude, "Most gladly I will rather boast in my infirmities, that the power of Christ may rest upon me." Are you glad about this as well?

Happy in the Midst of Suffering

It is good for me that I have been afflicted, that I may learn Your statutes.

PSALM 119:71

Scottish minister John Dickie (1823–1891) knew all about suffering. Most of his life he struggled with debilitating illnesses. While he was still young, a physician said he was sure to die. With the help of a very strict regimen, John was able to extend his life another 40 years, yet barely so. He was frail and could do little. The final eight years of his life were spent largely in bedridden seclusion.

In the face of such affliction, John could have chosen to wallow in bitterness and despair. Instead, the few breaths of health and energy he had were devoted to prayer and writing letters that spoke of God's unceasing goodness to him. He was well qualified, then, to pen these words:

"Suffering, however severe, never diminishes by one grain-weight the true happiness of any soul; that is when the sufferer accepts it in faith, and love, and unreserved resignation. It purifies the happiness, and increases it; but in no case does it abridge it."[4]

Though we may have no choice about suffering, we do have a choice about how we respond to it. Suffering and happiness *can* co-exist.

Good Results from Bad Circumstances

We know that all things work together for good to those who love God.

ROMANS 8:28

It was because Noah ignored the taunts of men for 120 years that the ark was built. It was because Joseph was a slave and prisoner that he eventually became the second-most powerful ruler over all Egypt and saved the people of Israel from death by famine.

It was because Ruth was willing to give up everything that she gained a good husband and became part of the family line of Jesus. It was because Esther was willing to perish that the nation of Israel was spared from annihilation. It was because Daniel was a captive that King Nebuchadnezzar of the mighty Babylonian Empire came to recognize God's greatness.

The Bible is filled with examples of those who endured great difficulties that, in the end, made good results possible. The supreme example, of course, is the Lord Jesus Christ. It is because He was willing to die that we are able to live—forever.

Yes, God is able to make "all things work together for good." May we be willing to endure!

Tested by Fire…for His Glory

You have been grieved by various trials, that the genuineness of your faith, being much more precious than gold that perishes, though it is tested by fire, may be found to praise, honor, and glory at the revelation of Jesus Christ.

1 PETER 1:6-7

It is the hot fires of affliction that refine our faith so as to make us stronger Christians. The proof of this is found all throughout God's Word. The lives of the great men and women of the Bible were shaped and molded—time and again—in the school of suffering. It was here that they learned painful yet precious lessons that could not be learned anywhere else—and the same holds true for us.

With every trial comes the resources to endure it. Yet our response to the trial can mean the difference between growing from it or suffering all the more. When we submit willingly, the burden is bearable. But when we resist God's work in us, we will find ourselves struggling against the burden in our own strength—only to discover it's utterly overwhelming.

We are able to grow from suffering only as long as we permit our loving heavenly Father to do His work unhindered. It is when we are humble, patient, and willing in life's trials that God is able to make us stronger, purer, and richer.

The Benefits of Trials

Blessed is the man who perseveres under trial,
because when he has stood the test, he will receive
the crown of life that God has promised to those
who love Him.

JAMES 1:12 NIV

As children of God, we have two basic choices about how we respond to our trials. We can complain about the difficulties they bring upon us, or we can thank our heavenly Father for the ways in which they refine us.

How can our problems turn out to our lasting good? One way is that they loosen our attachment to this world and turn our focus upon the things of heaven. Another is that they prompt us to more fervent prayer. Yet another is that they cause us to examine our hearts and make sure we haven't neglected some secret sin within. And then there's the fact affliction helps strengthen our faith. The soldier who has gained experience through increasingly intense battles is the one who becomes the most proficient warrior. Likewise for the Christian—the more our faith has been tried, the more mightily God can use us.

How much better it is to endure trials than to evade them! Pray that God will sanctify your sorrows…and use them for His divine purposes.

Growing from Affliction

Before I was afflicted I went astray, but now I keep your word.

PSALM 119:67

A short time of affliction can tell us more about our spiritual health than a long time of introspection when everything is going well.

It is when life becomes difficult that we become much more aware of whether our trust in God runs deep or is superficial. Whether our times of prayer have been consistent or infrequent. Whether we have truly let His Word fill our hearts to the point we remember His many assurances to us, or we've neglected to take the time we need for His Word to become our source of comfort.

Affliction has a way of nudging us closer to God as nothing else can. It produces within us a deeper longing for the Lord, a stronger fervency in prayer, a greater hunger for His Word.

Indeed, it is in the soil of affliction that some of our greatest spiritual growth takes place.

Why Does God Allow Evil?

Though He slay me, yet will I trust Him.

Job 13:15

Admittedly, Job 13:15 is not a promise, but rather a statement from one of the most well-known sufferers in all the Bible. Yet Job's words point us to some valuable lessons about trusting God when we are in the middle of tough circumstances.

We're familiar with the story: Satan comes before God and says, in essence, "The only reason Job is such a righteous man is because You are so good to him. Allow him to suffer, and surely he will curse You!" And thus begins one of the greatest mysteries in all Scripture—why God permits Satan to heap afflictions of unimaginable proportions upon Job.

Bible scholars and everyday Christians alike have long struggled with the questions raised by the events described in the book of Job. Why does God allow evil? Does evil's presence in this world mean He isn't really in control after all? Does it mean Satan has the power to wreak havoc, and the best God can do is minimize the damage?

For reasons known only to Him, God has chosen not to give us clear revelation on this, and the fact we have fallen, finite minds makes it extremely difficult—if not impossible—for us to fully piece together the answers. But these things we do know:

Yes, God is in control. Satan was unable to afflict Job without God's permission. Consider also that if God were not in control, then evil would be able to run *un*controlled. Things would be far, *far* worse than they are now.

And no, God doesn't just minimize the damage. In ways beyond our understanding, He can take that which was intended for evil and turn it to our ultimate benefit. We have the assurance of Romans 8:28, which says that "all things work together for good to those who love God." That's *all* things!

We also have the testimony of Joseph in the book of Genesis, where we read the story about how his brothers, out of jealousy, decide to rid themselves of him by selling him into slavery. This, in turn, leads to his being accused falsely of wrongdoing and ending up in prison.

But God miraculously uses these circumstances to ultimately make Joseph a ruler, alongside Pharaoh, over all Egypt. When famine strikes the land of Israel, Joseph's brothers find it necessary to go to Egypt to purchase food to stay alive. And it is because of Joseph's position in Egypt that eventually he is able to bring all his family and their relatives down to Egypt to preserve them from the famine, which by this time had spread to Egypt. When Joseph's brothers seek his forgiveness for their wicked deed against him, he says, "You meant evil against me; but God meant it for good, in order to bring it about as it is this day, to save many people alive" (Genesis 50:20).

Think about it: Joseph's brothers meant evil against *one man.* Yet God turned that around into good not just for Joseph, but for the *entire young nation of Israel,* which was preserved from death by famine as a result of God's orchestration of countless events behind the scenes.

When it comes to evil, God does not have His hands tied behind His back. Romans 8:28 and Genesis 50:20 tell us otherwise. God's perfect plan for our lives is firmly woven in and around any evil that might come our way, and He is somehow able to permit that which He hates to achieve what He loves.

Just because we are unable to comprehend how this is possible doesn't mean it's impossible. Rather than constrain ourselves by our inability to figure this out, we should free ourselves by resting in the truth that God's wisdom and ways are beyond our understanding. Romans 11:33 proclaims, "Oh, the depth of the riches both of the wisdom and knowledge of God! How unsearchable are His judgments and His ways past finding out!"

As God's children, our place is not to try to understand, but rather, to trust. Job recognized this. It's why he was able to say, "Though He slay me, yet will I trust Him."

Though we are unable to figure out why God allows evil, we do know with certainty how we should respond to it. We're to trust God, and believe that…

- He is in control.
- He has our best interests at heart.
- He will never allow us to face more than we can handle.
- He has already secured complete and lasting victory over evil.

He Hears Your Cry

Because God is the living God, He can hear;
because He is a loving God, He will hear;
because He is our covenant God,
He has bound Himself to hear.

C.H. SPURGEON

He Always Hears

Hear me, O LORD, for Your lovingkindness is good;
turn to me according to the multitude of Your
tender mercies. And do not hide Your face from
Your servant, for I am in trouble; hear me speedily.

PSALM 69:16

Even in the midst of trouble, we can say with confidence that God's "lovingkindness is good." And though we may not see them, we can count on His "tender mercies." These are certainties we can be sure of, no matter how dark the night around us.

Sometimes we are so preoccupied with our problems that we fail to notice God's care in the other areas of our life. Or, we fail to observe that our situation could be worse, and it isn't—thanks to the Lord's mercy.

When we appeal to God in our sorrows, we can know He will always hear us speedily. From our human perspective, when we don't see a quick response from God, we fear that He is ignoring us or has forgotten us. But that's not the case. He worked out His perfect solutions to every one of our dilemmas even before we were born (Psalm 139:16). Though we may never understand His reasons for delaying His response, we can always rest in the truths that He *does* love us and He *will* hear us.

He Knows Your Need

*You drew near on the day I called on You, and
said, "Do not fear!"*

LAMENTATIONS 3:57

When Abraham and Sarah rejected Hagar, their maid,
Hagar took her son and went into the wilderness. Lacking
food, water, and shelter, she cried out in despair, for she
was sure they would die. God heard her cry and said, "Fear
not, for God has heard" (Genesis 21:17).

When Elijah fled from the wicked queen Jezebel, he
was afraid and "prayed that he might die" (1 Kings 19:4).
God didn't answer that prayer. Instead, He provided Elijah
with food and much-needed rest.

No matter how desperate your situation, God hears
your cry. Both Hagar and Elijah found themselves in
extreme circumstances, and God met them at their point
of need. He will do the same for you too. If your prayers
have not been answered yet, it's not because God hasn't
heard. Remember that He has promised, "I will never leave
you nor forsake you" (Hebrews 13:5).

Don't ever give up. Wait patiently upon the Lord and
trust Him. He hears you, and He knows your need.

A Helper Who Hears and Saves

I will call upon God, and the LORD shall save me.
Evening and morning and at noon I will pray, and
cry aloud, and He shall hear my voice.

PSALM 55:16-17

There are many ways we can choose to respond to affliction. We can become frustrated, depressed, or angry. We can wallow in self-pity or point the finger of blame at others. But there is only one solution that truly works, that never fails. And that is to call upon God.

When it comes to being a helper, there is no one who is stronger, better, wiser. There is no one who is more compassionate, no one who is more able. That He will save you is not even a question. It's only a matter of how and when.

Because our understanding is limited, we might not perceive His hand at work. But this promise from Psalm 55 is absolute. God *will* hear, and He *will* save. Whether you call upon Him in the morning, at noon, or in the evening, He will listen to your voice.

Joy in the Midst of Persecution

*Vindicate me, O God, and plead my cause against
an ungodly nation; oh, deliver me from the
deceitful and unjust man!...Then I will go to the
altar of God, to God my exceeding joy.*

PSALM 43:1,4

It hurts when we are unjustly accused, mocked, or slandered. Though in our hearts we know we have done nothing wrong, still, we cannot help but become discouraged when we are attacked by people with evil intent.

When others hurt us, it's natural for us to ask God to vindicate and deliver us. Yet we shouldn't stop there. After all, deliverance might not come immediately. In fact, as Christians, we should *expect* mistreatment. Jesus said, "If they persecuted Me, they will also persecute you" (John 15:20).

So what can we do when we're under attack? As the psalmist said, "Go to the altar of God, to God my exceeding joy." Only God can give us joy in the midst of tribulation. Go into His presence and cling to Him. Dwell on *who* He is and *what* He has done for you, and you will find your heart lifted up.

When we are persecuted, the answer isn't to resent our enemies, but to rejoice in the Lord Himself.

You Are on His Heart

*Our total welfare is the constant
concern of God's heart.*

W.J.C. WHITE

He Never Forgets You

The LORD has been mindful of us; He will bless us.

PSALM 115:12

Though you may feel as if God has forgotten you, it will never happen. Nor is He ever so busy elsewhere that He doesn't have time to help you.

That Your heavenly Father has faithfully cared for you in the past reveals you are always on His heart. And His attention will never waver in the future. Psalm 34:15 reminds us that "the eyes of the LORD are on the righteous."

When problems arise in your life, don't interpret them as a sign that God has forgotten you. God didn't forget Abraham and Sarah as they waited decades for a child. Or Joseph as he spent years in slavery and prison in Egypt. Or Job when he lost all his children and livestock and endured agonizing illness.

The saints of the past are proof that, in God's hands, life's painful times can become life's growing times. They are also proof that His faithfulness never ceases. That God has a perfect record of being mindful assures us He will continue to be mindful.

His Love Is Constant

*Can a woman forget her nursing child, and not
have compassion on the son of her womb? Surely
they may forget, yet I will not forget you.*

ISAIAH 49:15

There is never a moment when you are not on God's
mind. His awareness of you is so perfect that He planned
every one of your days before you were born (Psalm
139:16). He knew every need you would have and how
to supply for it. He knew every crisis you would face and
how He could prepare and mature you to endure it. He
knew the struggles that would arise in your heart and how
to calm them—whether through counsel from His Word
or encouragement from fellow believers.

To think that God has forgotten you is to say He is
not all-knowing and to question His love for you. It is also
to doubt His tender assurance, "I will never leave you nor
forsake you" (Hebrews 13:5).

People may forget you, but God won't. His love for
you is constant. He has bound Himself to you not because
of what *you* do or say, but because of *His* promise to not
forget you.

Yes, you are always on His mind. Is He always on
yours?

He Knows Your Every Tear

You number my wanderings; put my tears into
Your bottle; are they not in Your book?

PSALM 56:8

Suffering has a way of heightening our loneliness. At times we may feel as if no one really understands or cares. After all, everyone has their own set of problems to deal with. Consequently, we tend to withdraw quietly from others. Deep down, we wish someone would notice and ask how we're feeling. And we yearn for a shoulder we can lean on.

As a Christian, you can take great comfort in knowing that your heavenly Father knows exactly how you feel. He knows your every pain, your every tear, your every wandering through the shadows of difficult circumstances. He numbers them all and records them in His book. That's how much He cares; none of them go unnoticed.

Though the people around you may be unaware, God is most definitely aware. He's closer to you than anyone else can be, and He cares more deeply about you than anyone else is able. Though you may be tempted to turn your back on Him when life isn't going well, don't. The best salve for pain is comfort, and you won't find any greater source of comfort than Him.

God Is Watching over You

The LORD is my rock and my fortress and my deliverer; My God, my strength, in whom I will trust.

PSALM 18:2

In the span of a few short words, David pens an incisive portrait of God and all that He is to us. He is our rock—a firm foundation upon which we can stand and never be moved. He is our fortress—a safe shelter in which we can hide and be protected. He is our deliverer—when all is hopeless and we have no answers, He comes alongside us and sets us free.

He is our God—this alone says a lot! He is faithful, unchanging, and perfect. He knows everything, sees everything, and is sovereign over everything. What more could we want? And He is our strength—we who are weak and vulnerable have a source of power and confidence.

But none of this means anything if we don't trust Him. It is only when we exercise faith in God that we can know and experience all He has to offer to us.

Are you trusting Him today?

He Is Everything You Need

*Affliction is sanctified when we are made
to feel that nothing can satisfy us but God,
and when we actually wait upon God, and
rely on Him as our only hope.*

JAMES W. ALEXANDER

Hoping in God Alone

I will cry out to God Most High, to God who performs all things for me.

PSALM 57:2

We humans can be stubborn sometimes.

When difficulties come our way, rather than seek God's help, we try to tackle them on our own. Or we respond to negative circumstances by becoming angry at God rather than drawing closer to Him. Either way, we tell God, in essence, "No thanks. I don't need Your help. You allowed me to get into this mess, and I'll get out on my own."

But a look to Scripture reminds us that God is all-wise, all-powerful, and that He loves us with a perfect love. He cares about us more than we know, and He is far more capable than we are. If there's anyone who wants to and is able to pull us through the hard times and forge good results from them, it's Him.

Have you ever considered that sometimes God allows us into situations that give us no alternative but to completely depend upon Him? Every trial we experience is an opportunity to make sure our hope is anchored in the right place. So when we cry out, may it be to Him "who performs all things." He can help you.

Victory over the Impossible

I will be with you. I will not leave you nor forsake you.

JOSHUA 1:5

Things looked very grim for the Israelites.

As they stood on the shore opposite the Promised Land, the mighty city-fortress of Jericho towered before them. Behind the massive walls was a powerful, menacing army. From a logistical standpoint, Israel did not stand a chance.

Except for the fact God was on Israel's side. God promised He would not fail His people, and He didn't. The victory was so astounding that only He could get the credit. That which was impossible for humans was not impossible for God.

What enemy rises before you? What has filled your heart with fear and robbed you of your confidence?

Your heavenly Father will never leave you to face your problems alone. And it doesn't matter how great those problems are—God is greater. In Him, you have every resource you need.

Everything We Could Ever Want

Who is God, except the LORD? And who is a rock, except our God?

PSALM 18:31

Nothing compares to having God at our side as we walk through life.

No one can help carry our burden as He can. No one can understand our pain as He can. No one can overrule our circumstances as He can. No one can forge beauty out of hardship as He can. No one can see and prepare us for the future as He can. And no one can deliver us from temptation and evil as He can.

Because He is a rock, we can fix our hopes upon Him and not worry that they will be shattered. We can place our trust in Him and not be anxious that He will change His mind. We can stand firm in Him and not be shaken by life's problems. We can rest in the assurance that He is steadfast, and that nothing will thwart His plans.

Yes, God is everything we could ever want!

Freedom from Anxiety

*The beginning of anxiety is the end of faith,
And the beginning of true faith is the end
of anxiety.*

GEORGE MÜLLER

One Day at a Time

Do not worry about tomorrow, for tomorrow will worry about its own things. Sufficient for the day is its own trouble.

MATTHEW 6:34

Worry does not lessen our suffering. Nor does it give us the strength we need to shoulder our burdens. Rather, it robs us of the time and energy we need for dealing with today.

Worry has a way of getting us to imagine troubles that do not yet exist—troubles that may never come. We should be grateful, then, that God has hidden the future from us. He mercifully commands us not to worry about what seems to be our lack for the next day, but to rest in His provision for this day.

To us, our future may seem dark and murky, but to our heavenly Father, it's very clear. He knows exactly what is coming, and He is already prepared to give us the help we need at the time we need it—not before.

Are you worried about tomorrow? Give your anxiety to God, for He is already there.

Resting in His Care

Cast all your anxiety on him because he cares for you.

1 PETER 5:7 NIV

No matter how heavy our burden or urgent our need, God's grace will always be sufficient. He will never allow a trial to go beyond what we can handle. He will never allow a difficult circumstance to enter our lives before the right time. And He will never leave us without the resources we need in order to endure.

As we enter into a problem, we often become filled with anxiety because we don't know the ultimate outcome. We cannot see ahead, which forces us to live just one day at a time. And that's exactly what God wants. We are to walk in humble dependence and total trust, knowing that God's grace is sufficient for today, and that He will supply our need for today.

When we fall into the trap of worrying about tomorrow, we'll find ourselves using today's provision and grace against tomorrow's problems. Let's not run ahead of God. Rather, let's stay in step with Him…and rest in His tender care.

Where to Find Peace

Great peace have those who love your law; and nothing causes them to stumble.

PSALM 119:165

The truths of God's Word can give us a peace as nothing else can. It is filled to overflowing with assurances of God's protective love and care for us, with accounts of God's watchfulness and provision for His people, with affirmations of God's faithfulness to keep His promises. God's Word confirms He has never failed His children in the past, and it testifies He will never fail them in the future.

The more richly God's Word dwells in us, the more peace we will experience in the trials of life. The more His truth resides in our hearts, the more prepared we are for suffering. The more familiar we are with His truths, the more able we are to resist the tempter's lies. One way Satan tries to rob us of our peace is to get us to doubt God's Word, or to struggle with that which we don't understand.

But in the times when we don't know what is happening to us or why, we do know we can trust God. His Word reveals Him to be unchanging, faithful, and true. And the more familiar we are with these traits of our heavenly Father, the greater our peace will be in difficult circumstances.

Letting God Do His Work

Our soul waits for the LORD; He is our help and our shield.

PSALM 33:20

If only we would wait upon God in all things! So often we run ahead of Him, impatient for results. We try to resolve life's problems in our own power and timing instead of God's.

Yes, it's tough to wait when we're hurting and there's no end in sight. We become frustrated and anxious, wishing for an immediate solution. But the Bible tells us to wait. We are to...

- ❧ wait upon God in prayer
- ❧ wait upon God with patience
- ❧ wait upon God with trust
- ❧ wait upon God for His guidance

To wait upon God does not mean giving up in passive resignation. Rather, it means offering yourself up in active surrender. It's not saying, "I guess I have no choice but to be yanked along." It's saying, "Here I am. Do whatever You desire in me."

Wait upon God, and you will never be disappointed. He is your help and your shield; He will take care of you.

Your Pain Has Purpose

*Affliction is the school in which
great virtues are acquired,
in which great characters are formed.*

HANNAH MORE

Growing a Stronger Faith

The God of all grace...after you have suffered a little while, will himself restore you and make you strong, firm and steadfast.

1 PETER 5:10 NIV

Have you ever wished for stronger faith—the kind that is not easily shaken when life gets difficult? Strong faith is a wonderful thing. But what is it that makes a person's faith more enduring? You probably won't like the answer: adversity.

Adversity is to faith what exercise is to the body. Only when you consistently exert your muscles do they develop. And only when you push your body past its limits does it reach new levels of strength.

The same is true about faith. It's only as we persevere through increasingly difficult trials that our faith grows stronger. Prosperity rarely leads to an increase in faith the way suffering does.

While facing adversity is never easy, we can take comfort in knowing that God will never give us more than we can handle. He is a compassionate Father who knows our limits and is always ready to help.

According to God's Plan

*This man was handed over to you by God's set
purpose and foreknowledge; and you with the help
of wicked men, put him to death by nailing him to
the cross.*

ACTS 2:23 NIV

Our suffering is never random or meaningless. It may
seem that way on this side of heaven, but from God's
perspective, it all makes sense and has purpose.

For example, the people who condemned Christ and
put Him to death thought they were in full control of what
they were doing. They paid one of the disciples to betray
Him, and they hired witnesses who were willing to make
false charges against Him. Then they pressured Pilate, the
Roman governor, into having Jesus crucified. In short,
Jesus' enemies had their way. Or so they thought.

Acts 2:23 says God ordained that all this would
happen. The Divine Director was still in control behind
the scenes of this human drama. That which was evil was
used by God to bring about good.

The same is true about our suffering. God foresees
all our pain and uses it for our good. Though we might
not understand how that is possible, we can trust Him,
because with Him, everything is possible.

God's Work in Us

He who has begun a good work in you will complete it until the day of Jesus Christ.

PHILIPPIANS 1:6

In every trial we encounter, God is for us, not against us. He does not intend for trials to crush or defeat us. Rather, He uses affliction to build within us qualities that we might otherwise not cultivate.

Before every trial, God *prepares* us. He equips us with wisdom from His Word, guidance from His Holy Spirit, and the interceding ministry of His Son.

In the *midst* of every trial, God *refines* us. He purges away that which is impure and undesirable, thus making us more holy and useful.

As a *result* of every trial, God *strengthens* us. As we become more experienced and spiritually mature, God is able to use us for greater works.

In these ways, trials are a part of the "good work" God does in us to make us more complete!

Refined by the Master

When He has tested me, I shall come forth as gold.

JOB 23:10

The spiritual strength we need in order to persevere through trials is developed not when the seas of life are calm, but when they are rough and stormy. It is in the midst of difficult circumstances that we develop the skills necessary to keep the ship afloat and on course without capsizing or crashing against deadly cliffs.

Life's trials, then, serve a definite purpose. Our past and current afflictions are the tests that provide us with the wisdom, confidence, and strength we need for successfully overcoming future tribulations.

As much as we would rather remove all pain and suffering from our lives, it's far better that we allow the Lord to test and teach us. For then, when troubles come, He can use us and work through us to bring some ultimate and eternal good out of a temporary and earthly problem. And in the end, we will "come forth as gold." We will have been refined by the Master Himself.

God is ready to work through you. Are you ready to let Him?

84

Joy in the Midst of Trials

Count it all joy when you fall into various trials, knowing that the testing of your faith produces patience.

JAMES 1:2-3

Here within these verses we find the secret to responding with joy anytime life gets rough. James is not telling us to manufacture joy out of nothing. He's not talking about plastering a fake smile over our problems.

The secret to possessing joy is to look ahead, with faith, at the end result of our trials. James tells us that the testing of our faith "produces patience." Patience here speaks of inner strength, of endurance, of deeper trust in God. It is in the school of difficult circumstances we grow these valuable qualities. And every trial we face is another opportunity to grow even more.

From where can we get joy, then? From *looking ahead* to the stronger person we will become. And from *looking upward* to the God who promises to uphold and sustain us.

Trials help us grow and bring us closer to God. Though the journey is never easy, upon reaching our destination, we will see that it was all worthwhile.

God's Promise to Those Who Love Him

We know that all things work together for good to those who love God.

ROMANS 8:28

Romans 8:28 is perhaps one of the most frequently quoted verses in the Bible...and one of the more misunderstood passages.

What it's not saying: It's not saying *all* things are good. It's not saying that bad things will somehow *become* good. And it's not saying our lives will be free of trouble, always filled with good.

What it is saying: God has the power to somehow, in ways we don't understand, take the challenges, the difficulties, the pains of life, and forge beautiful results from them. These results can include greater patience, stronger faith, deeper trust, purer motives, truer humility, nobler desires, and a more God-centered life.

Bad will still happen. But somewhere, somehow, good will be drawn out of it. That's God's promise to those who love Him.[5]

Yielding Fully to God

*In shunning a trial we are seeking
to avoid a blessing.*

C.H. SPURGEON

Clinging to the Lord Alone

*Everywhere and in all things I have learned both
to be full and to be hungry, both to abound and to
suffer need. I can do all things through Christ who
strengthens me.*

PHILIPPIANS 4:12-13

"If only my circumstances were different, I would be
so much happier," we say.

We wish for a better job, house, or car. We complain
about our looks, our limitations, our lot in life. Perhaps
our marriage has encountered difficulties, our children
make parenting a challenge, or our health is declining.
Or perhaps our lives have been shattered in some truly
unimaginable way and, in bewilderment, we cry out, "God,
why did You allow this to happen to me?"

And what if we can't change our circumstance? That
often leaves us feeling helpless. And hopeless. That's exactly
where God wants us—at the point of total dependence
upon Him. Only He can give us what it takes to persevere
when life is terribly messed up.

Even when Paul was hungry and suffering, he could
still say, "I can do all things through Christ who strengthens
me." Why? Because he had learned the power of letting go
of *all* circumstances and clinging to God *alone*.

The Blessing of Total Surrender

Humble yourselves in the sight of the Lord, and He will lift you up.

JAMES 4:10

The greatest and most difficult lesson of the Christian life is to surrender ourselves to our heavenly Father and say, "Not my will, but Yours be done."

Christ's death on the cross was the most amazing example of such surrender the universe has ever witnessed. The night before, He told His Father, "Not as I will, but as You will" (Matthew 26:39). The innocent Lamb of God who did no wrong paid an unimaginably horrible price for the sins of the world. His was the ultimate self-sacrifice.

Was it all worthwhile? Absolutely! The pain and humiliation were excruciating, but the end result is that God "highly exalted Him" (Philippians 2:9)—and that *we* can be blessed "with *every* spiritual blessing in the heavenly places in Christ" (Ephesians 1:3).

Such total surrender is never easy. But nothing pleases God more than to hear His children say, "Father, if it is Your will for me to experience this trial, please show me how to endure it."

Are you willing?

All Sufficiency in All Things

*To have any proper view of the divine
mercy, we should consider who and what
He is, of whom it is predicated; how
high, how great, how all-sufficient, how
independent, and infinite in perpetual bliss.*

JAMES W. ALEXANDER

He Fulfills Our Every Need

My God shall supply all your need according to His riches in glory by Christ Jesus.

PHILIPPIANS 4:19

When we think of God supplying for our needs, typically we think in terms of physical provision. But notice that Philippians 4:19 uses the word *all*. This promise applies to more than just food, clothing, and shelter.

Are you lacking peace? Your heavenly Father can give the kind that surpasses all understanding. Rest? He can make you to lie down in green pastures. Wisdom? He is ready to give it—we need only to ask. Assurance? He who has never failed any of His children will not fail you. Hope? He has given us many glimpses of the wonderful future ahead of us, reminding us that our earthly tribulations are temporary. Victory over temptation? He has empowered us and made a way of escape, so if we fall, we can only blame ourselves.

Whatever your true needs, He will supply them— "according to His riches in glory." God's storehouses cannot be exhausted. He is more than generous; He gives more than abundantly. By the world's measure we may be poor, but by God's measure we are rich…because He has supplied *all* our needs.

More Than Enough Grace

*My grace is sufficient for you, for My strength is
made perfect in weakness.*

2 CORINTHIANS 12:9

Is there ever a problem or trial so great that it exceeds
the limits of God's grace for us?

The much-loved preacher Charles Spurgeon answered
that question with three illustrations, saying, "It's as if a tiny
fish, being very thirsty, was troubled with fear of drinking
the river dry, and the Thames River said to him, 'Poor
little fish, my stream is sufficient for you.' Put one mouse
in all the granaries of Egypt when they were fullest after
seven years of plenty, and imagine the mouse complaining
it might die of famine. 'Cheer up,' says Pharaoh, 'poor
mouse, my granaries are sufficient for you.' Imagine a
man standing on a mountain and saying, 'I am afraid I
will ultimately inhale all the oxygen that surrounds the
globe.' And the earth replies, 'My atmosphere is sufficient
for you.'" [6]

In every need we have, God's grace is more than
sufficient. May we never fear that God's provision and
help will ever run out!

Have We Noticed?

The LORD upholds all who fall, and raises up all who are bowed down.

PSALM 145:14

In the same way that we are unable to see the stars in the heavens when the sun is shining brightly, we seldom notice God's compassion when everything in life is going smoothly. Only in the darkness of night are we able to even see the stars—and it is in the darkest hour of night that the stars shine their brightest. Similarly, it's in the dark moments of life that God's care becomes more noticeable to us. And it's in the most difficult times we experience the greatest measure of His comfort.

He has promised that when we are weak, His grace will be fully sufficient and His strength will shine forth (2 Corinthians 12:9). And He has promised that when we are suffering, His comfort will abound (2 Corinthians 1:3-5).

It is because of our trials that we become more intimately acquainted with God's love, grace, and power. It is through our hurts we see Him care for us in ways we would never see otherwise. And the more intense our affliction, the more abundantly He provides in order to meet our need.

Secure in God

I am the LORD your God.

JOEL 2:27

When we are deeply unsettled and feeling unsure about our lot in life, the greatest comfort we have is that we can be sure about God.

Temptations may plague us, and doubts may assail us. Questions may haunt us, and fear may disturb us. We may even reach the point of questioning God's existence, or feel as though He is powerless to help us.

Yet no matter how our circumstances make us feel, there is *nothing* that can threaten the certainty of who God is and the security of our relationship with Him. To hear Him say, "I am the LORD your God" can give us a sense of restful calm and confidence even in the worst of earthly disasters.

God is God, and nothing can change that. He has committed Himself to caring for you. Doesn't that make you feel secure?

The God of All Comfort

*All the compassions of all the tender fathers
in the world compared with the tender
mercies of our God would be but as a
candle to the sun or a drop to the ocean.*

MATTHEW HENRY

The Promise of His Presence

*The LORD, He is the One who goes before you. He
will be with you, He will not leave you nor forsake
you; do not fear nor be dismayed.*

DEUTERONOMY 31:8

In the times when you find yourself in need of extra-
strength assurance, Deuteronomy 31:8 is an especially
comforting passage.

God goes before you. No matter what path you walk,
God has already been on it. Which means He knows
exactly what you are facing. It also means that nothing
can hinder you, for He is clearing the way for you to
follow in His steps.

God stays with you. You will never face a trial alone;
God is your constant companion. The fact that God is
present doesn't mean suffering will be absent. Rather, His
presence assures that you will have *all* His resources at
your disposal in your time of need.

As the wonderful hymn says,

> *Fear not, I am with thee; O be not dismayed,*
> *For I am thy God, and will still give thee aid;*
> *I'll strengthen thee, help thee, and cause thee to stand,*
> *Upheld by my righteous, omnipotent hand.*[7]

God Is Near

The LORD is near to all who call upon Him, to all who call upon Him in truth.

PSALM 145:18

There is nothing shallow about God's compassion in the midst of your afflictions. He isn't one to give quick pats on the back and artificial "cheer up" pep talks. God isn't like a friend who merely checks in on you every now and then. No, He is with you for the long haul. He is intimately involved in your life. He knows your every pain, and He is by your side at all times to help you persevere.

Nor does God play favorites. He is near to *all* who call upon Him. Don't think you need to earn points in order to secure His help. And don't assume that problems have come your way because you did something wrong. All Christians experience trials.

Yet to "call upon Him" when life gets rough means exercising faith on your part. Are you willing to lean upon Him, to trust Him completely? And to "call upon Him in truth" is to have a sincere and right heart when you bring your pleas to Him. Are you seeking your own gain, or His glory?

Always Comforting

Blessed be...the Father of mercies and God of all comfort, who comforts us in all our tribulation, that we may be able to comfort those who are in any trouble, with the comfort with which we ourselves are comforted by God.

2 CORINTHIANS 1:3-4

These verses are literally overflowing with encouraging truths we can cling to when we suffer.

Our Father is the God of all comfort. God's mercy and compassion are an inextricable part of His nature. They are part of who He is. What's more, He is the God of *all* comfort. He can meet every need of every believer in every circumstance.

Our Father comforts us in all our tribulation. That's *all* our afflictions. In the original Greek text, we're told that God is "always comforting." His care for us never diminishes. Though our faulty human perceptions may suggest God has abandoned us, Scripture says otherwise.

Our Father enables us to bring comfort to others. When we experience God's comfort, we can then pass it on to others who hurt. Such comfort is powerful because we received it from the Master Comforter Himself.

Comfort for Life's Hurts

As one whom his mother comforts, so I will comfort you.

ISAIAH 66:13

Humanly speaking, a mother's comfort is the best kind there is. Nothing can heal a child's hurts better than a mother's touch, kindness, words, gentleness, and sympathy. When it comes to comfort, no one does it better than a mom.

Scripture likens God's comfort to that of a mother. When we are in pain, He invites us warmly into His presence and lavishes compassion on us. He listens tenderly to our cries and wipes away our tears. He knows best how to quiet and reassure our frightened hearts. He will not mock our weakness as some people might. Rather, He delights in bearing our griefs with us.

That's why it doesn't make sense to shake your fist at God when affliction comes. To do so is to resist the love of the One who can comfort you best. In times of anguish, then, may you rush into His arms with haste, and seek His motherly care. Let Him do what only He can do.

A Guide You Can Trust

*If God sends us on stony paths He will
provide us with strong shoes.*

ALEXANDER MACLAREN

Safe in the Shepherd's Care

Though I walk through the valley of the shadow of death, I will fear no evil; for You are with me; Your rod and Your staff, they comfort me.

PSALM 23:4

In Israel, when shepherds took their sheep from the winter lowlands to the summer highlands, they had to travel through canyons that were inhabited by dangerous animals and were at risk of floods from sudden storms. The rough terrain meant the sheep were also vulnerable to serious or fatal injuries. For these reasons a good shepherd stayed close to his sheep the whole journey. With the shepherd nearby, the sheep had no reason to be afraid.

Life has its difficult terrain as well, with danger and uncertainties lurking in the shadows. Yet we have no reason to be afraid. Why? Because our Lord, the Great Shepherd, is with us.

Notice the psalmist did not say, "I will fear no evil *after* I am out of the valley." Rather, he said, "I will fear no evil even *while* I am in this valley." Why? "For You are with me." It is God's presence that gives us true comfort, not the absence of affliction.

No matter how rough the journey, the Great Shepherd is with you. He will keep you safe.

He Directs Our Every Step

The LORD will guide you continually.

ISAIAH 58:11

At times, the storms of life are so dark that we cannot see more than a step or two ahead of us. We move onward with hesitation because the ground is treacherous, and we're not sure of what lies ahead.

In such times of uncertainty, we have a Guide who knows the way. We need only to cry out to Him, and He will direct us. He will hold on to us firmly so we do not fall.

And this guidance is continual! It is available every moment…every hour…every day. Our Guide is always with us, always ready to lead. There is no circumstance so great, no trial so difficult, no crisis so overwhelming that our Father is unable to lead us to safety.

Though we cannot see what's ahead in the future, God can. Though we have no control over our circumstances, God does. Won't you yield to His leading?

Our Lifelong Guide

He will be our guide even to death.

PSALM 48:14

When climbing over mountain ranges full of dangerous precipices and hazardous trails that lead to nowhere, it is wise to have a guide who knows the way and can lead us to our destination safely.

And when it comes to journeying over the mountains of life, God has promised to be our Guide. He already knows what lies ahead. He knows where to find the safe meadows and the quiet streams. When we follow Him, we will stay on safe paths and not lose our way.

And though we cannot see what lies over the ridge into tomorrow, we do not need to worry, for God has already been there. He knows the future, and is in control of it.

Our heavenly Father promises to guide us "even to death." Even in life's final moments—no matter how painful and despairing—He stays with us to comfort and lead us.

Restoring Your Hope

*True hope is inadvertent. It does not come
from searching for hope. It grows out of two
basic convictions: that God is in charge and
that He intervenes.*

LLOYD JOHN OGILVIE

The Power of Hope

Happy is he...whose hope is in the LORD his God.

PSALM 146:5

If there is any one thing that can help sustain us through life's trials, it is hope. Biblical hope is not a mere optimism or cheerfulness in spite of our circumstances. Rather, it is a deep-seated confidence that God will orchestrate all things in our lives so they work out for our ultimate good.

It is hope that helps take our eyes off the pain of the moment and focus them instead on who God is and what He can do. It is hope that enables us to look beyond our inability and trust His ability. It is hope that reminds us our mortal bodies will one day become immortal.

Hope tells us there is coming a day when we will know perfect and unending peace, joy, and happiness. When we allow hope to reside in our hearts, it makes the cares of this world grow dimmer and the treasures awaiting us in heaven grow brighter.

Hope is not just wishful thinking. God *can* do and *will* do what He promises. The greater your confidence in that truth, the greater the hope you will know.

A Heart of Thanks
Is a Heart of Hope

Why art you cast down, O my soul?…Hope in God, for I shall yet praise Him for the help of His countenance.

PSALM 42:5

No matter how bad life becomes, we always have blessings for which we can thank God.

The more we fill our heart with the sunshine of thanks, the less room remains for the gloom of despair. At first we may find it hard to find reasons to thank God. But as Christians, a very important one is thankfulness we are going to heaven, and not hell. Another is thankfulness that, in spite of our sins, God chose to save us and to love us with an everlasting love.

Then there are all the past mercies God has shown us—in the form of physical provisions, spiritual nourishment, family, friends, fellow believers. Our present mercies include the gifts of His Word to guide us, His Spirit to comfort us, and His love to sustain us. And our future mercies are beyond what we can imagine—all the riches that await us in eternity!

Give thanks…and you'll find your heart lifted up in hope.

Don't Give Up

Weeping may endure for a night, but joy comes in the morning.

PSALM 30:5

Has your suffering reached the point where you have thought about giving up on God? Or asking Him to leave you alone?

Consider your options. If you give up on God, where are you going to go? Who can you turn to for help? Ultimately, there are only two paths available. You can depend on either human resources or divine ones. And any help you might receive from people will never come close to that which God can do for you.

So giving up on God doesn't seem such an attractive option, does it?

No matter how many things are going wrong in your life, as a Christian, you will always have these things going right for you: *God loves you. Nothing can separate you from Him. He will never leave you. And He has an inheritance waiting in heaven for you.*

Don't wander from God. If you stay close to Him all through the darkness, then you'll find yourself close to Him when daybreak finally comes.

Trusting His Goodness

You are good, and do good; teach me Your statutes.

Psalm 119:68

Our emotions are powerful, and Satan knows that. He knows that when we become discouraged, we tend to listen to our negative feelings and get dragged down by them. That's what he wants.

We think, *I'm a failure. Why do I even bother? Nothing ever goes right anyway.* Or we vent: *God, where are You? Why aren't You listening to my cries for help?* And we let our feelings suck us downward into the vortex of pity and forget what we know to be true about God: He is good. He loves us. He's in control. He promises to never abandon us.

Negative feelings have a way of distorting positive truths. That's why, when we're feeling down, the best remedy is to focus our minds on God's truths and not trust our feelings.

Feelings change all the time; God's truth never changes. Where are you placing your trust?

No Problem Too Great

God raises the level of the impossible.

CORRIE TEN BOOM

A Needed Perspective

You are great, and do wondrous things; You alone are God.

PSALM 86:10

When life isn't going well, it helps to remember...

Who God Is. He's the Creator. A Father. A Rock. A Deliverer. A King. A Fortress. A Shield. A Tower of Strength. A Savior. An Advocate. The Almighty. The Most High God. The Lord of all the Earth.

The attributes of God. He is perfect. Eternal. Sovereign. Holy. Righteous. Unchanging. All-wise. All-powerful. All-knowing. All-present. Merciful. Faithful. Good. Loving. Kind. Patient. Just. Personal. Self-sufficient. Self-existent.

Who Jesus is. The Good Shepherd. The Holy One. Immanuel—God with us. Lamb of God. Man of Sorrows. Mediator. Messiah. Prince of Peace. Savior. The Light. The Truth. The King of kings and Lord of lords.

The character of Jesus. He humbled Himself. Came to serve. Loved the unlovely. Healed sickness. Forgave sins. Showed compassion. Resisted temptation. Washed feet. Turned the other cheek. Obeyed to the point of death.

This is the One who loves and cares for you in the midst of every trial. Yes, He is great, and He does wonderful things.

Setting Our Minds on God

*It is God who arms me with strength, and makes
my way perfect.*

PSALM 18:32

When we find ourselves feeling discouraged we often look to others to help lift us up, or we hope for better circumstances. Yet neither option is a lasting solution. People are fallible and frequently will disappoint us. And circumstances are unpredictable and usually beyond our control. The secret to experiencing consistent joy no matter how difficult life gets is to set our minds on what we know to be true about God. For example…

God never changes. That means His love for you will never end. Nor His mercy. Nor His provision.

God is just. Those who have treated you unfairly will not get away with it. Ultimately, all sin and injustice will be punished.

God is patient. He won't give up on you. He is committed to completing the work He began in you.

It's truths like these—truths about God Himself—that are a source of real and permanent assurance when life gets rough. The more we know Him, the more joy we'll experience.

Sin, Guilt, and Forgiveness

My sin, O, the bliss of this glorious thought,
My sin not in part but the whole,
Is nailed to the cross and I bear it no more,
Praise the Lord, praise the Lord, O my soul!

HORATIO G. SPAFFORD
"IT IS WELL WITH MY SOUL"

The Benefits of Correction

No chastening seems to be joyful for the present,
but painful; nevertheless, afterward it yields the
peaceable fruit of righteousness to those who have
been trained by it.

Hebrews 12:11

Puritan Thomas Brooks wisely observed that "God's house of correction is His school of instruction."[8] At times God will allow us to experience trials so that He can impress an important truth or lesson upon our heart.

The Bible affirms this. For example, God used Moses' 40-year exile in the desert to strengthen his character and prepare him for delivering the Israelites from Egypt. And God used a "thorn in the flesh" to teach Paul that His grace was sufficient for his every need (2 Corinthians 12:9).

No difficulty in life is without reason. In God's loving hands, the hammer and chisel of affliction have the potential to chip away that which is undesirable and to shape that which remains—in the same way a sculptor chips away at a rough rock to transform it into a work of art.

Are you a willing and patient learner? Though the results may be long in coming, we can know they are always for our best.

Freedom from Guilt

If we confess our sins, He is faithful and just to for-
give us our sins and to cleanse us from all unrigh-
teousness.

1 JOHN 1:9

Sin has a way of pulling us downward even after
the act itself is long past. Our hearts are weighed heavy
with guilt; our consciences are unable to rest at night.
We've made a poor choice—again. And we've disappointed
God—again. We are so frustrated that even when we ask
God to forgive us, we are unable to forgive ourselves.

Sometimes we wallow in our guilt, allowing it to
become depression or despair. And with the apostle Paul
we say, "O wretched man that I am! Who will deliver me
from this body of death?" (Romans 7:24).

Yet when we have genuinely repented of our wrong
and asked our Father's forgiveness, He is "faithful and just
to forgive us" (1 John 1:9).

And if we have asked God's forgiveness, we have no
reason to feel guilty any longer. As Romans 8:1 says, there
is "no condemnation to those who are in Christ Jesus." Are
you condemning yourself for a past sin already surrendered
to God? Let it go. Rest in His forgiveness. And thank Jesus
for having freed you from the bondage of sin.

Forever Forgiven

He will not always strive with us, nor will He keep
His anger forever.

PSALM 103:9

At times a parent finds it necessary to discipline a child. Though it is never easy to give out punishment, a wise and loving mom or dad will do what is necessary to teach a child to make right choices in life.

As it is between a parent and child, so it is between our heavenly Father and us. No punishment is pleasant when it comes. Nor does God delight in rebuking us. But He does so out of love and concern.

Thankfully, one of the Holy Spirit's ministries is to convict our hearts when we disobey God. The Spirit lets us know when we have grieved the Lord and calls attention to our need to turn away from sin and seek forgiveness. And we can rejoice in knowing that God is faithful to forgive—He will not keep His anger forever. He is not like us humans, who hold grudges and seek vengeance. God revealed the infinite greatness of His love for us in the price He paid at the cross, and it is a love that will never change.

With God, when all is forgiven, it is truly forgiven.

When God Is Silent

Never was a faithful prayer lost. Some prayers have a longer voyage than others, but then they return with their richer lading at last, so that the praying soul is a gainer by waiting for an answer.

WILLIAM GURNALL

Trusting God Even
When There's No Answer

Show Your marvelous lovingkindness by Your right hand, O You who save those who trust in You.

PSALM 17:7

Why is God sometimes silent in the midst of our suffering? Why is it that even when we pray with the right motives and seek that which seems good, there is no answer?

We can take comfort in knowing that no less than Elijah and the apostle Paul—among the other great saints of the past—didn't have all their prayers answered. Receiving a response from God has nothing to do with your spiritual stature. God doesn't play favorites. Rather, He answers prayers according to His master plan for our lives.

It is in the times God does not answer that we have an opportunity to say, "Father, I don't understand, but I trust You." It is this kind of dependence and faith that God desires to build in us.

When it seems as though God is not hearing us, our perspective should not be, "What can I do to get my prayer answered?" but rather, "What might God be doing through this to draw me closer to Him and make me more useful to Him?"

Keep Praying

*This is the confidence that we have in Him, that if
we ask anything according to His will, He hears us.*

1 JOHN 5:14

When our prayers aren't answered, sometimes our
eventual response is to stop praying. We figure God isn't
going to respond, so we give up. But what if the reason
God hasn't answered is because the time is not yet right?
Or the request isn't the right one? Or what if He *has*
answered and we just haven't recognized it?

God's timing and His ways may be different from
what we hope for because He can see the big picture and
we can't. So rather than ask Him to answer according to
our desires, we ought to pray that He answer according
to His.

When it comes to unanswered prayer, rather than
doubt God's wisdom, we should question our own. Is it
possible we're somehow limiting God?

When God doesn't answer, that doesn't mean it's time
to give up. Instead, keep praying. Pray to have a teachable
and willing heart. Pray that you will be a vessel God can
use. And pray for God to fulfill His plan even though you
don't understand it.

He Hears Your Prayers

The LORD has heard my supplication; the LORD will receive my prayer.

PSALM 6:9

Your prayers will never fall to the ground unheard. We have a King willing to hear all our petitions. He is not like a person who, depending on his or her mood, may or may not listen to us. No, He promises to hear us and receive our prayers—every one of them.

Of course, we cannot assume His acceptance of our prayers means He will answer in the way we want Him to. We must trust Him for the time and the manner in which He will respond. He knows our needs better than we do, and He has our best interests at heart.

Are you doubting whether God hears you? Doubt no more. His promise to hear means we can have full confidence. And when the answer is delayed or seems uncertain, the key is not to increase the volume of our prayers, but to increase the level of our trust. If you find yourself restless, it's probably because you are unsure that God hears. Surrender your anxieties and believe His promise…and you will know rest.

God's Invitation to You

*Call to me, and I will answer you, and show you
great and mighty things, which you do not know.*

JEREMIAH 33:3

Call to me! This is no halfhearted invitation. God urges us to pray—not timidly, but boldly. Not hesitantly, but confidently. When we hurt, our tendency is to withdraw, to shy away. But our heavenly Father welcomes us with open arms, assuring us of His attention and concern. Yes, He hears our prayers.

And He will answer as well. Perhaps not in the way we want or expect. In His love, He wants only what is best for us, and in His knowledge, He knows what is best for us. So whatever His answer, it is great and mighty because, in the long run, it is what we need most and what will glorify Him most.

Remember that when it comes to answering our prayers, God has the entire universe at His disposal. He can make use of whatever He needs, and nothing is too hard for Him to do.

Are you calling to Him? God is eager to hear you. May you be eager to speak to Him!

Learning from Jesus

For as long as sovereigns have reigned, citizens have been asked to sacrifice for king and country—their lands, their money, their children. But this king stepped from the merriment of His palace, abandoned the cheery fireplace and the spread table, resigned His luxuries and lands, and set out to perish for His citizens.

JONI EARECKSON TADA

Jesus' Example to Us

Consider [Jesus] who endured such opposition from sinful men, so that you will not grow weary and lose heart.

HEBREWS 12:3

Our dear Lord Jesus could easily have escaped the most painful of the earthly afflictions He suffered, but He chose not to. When He was arrested by the enemies who would murder Him upon the cross, He did not resist—even though He could have prayed to the Father for the help of "more than twelve legions of angels" (Matthew 26:53).

Jesus did not ask for angelic protection. He said, "How then would the Scriptures be fulfilled that say it must happen in this way?" (verse 54). For Him to evade the cross would have meant that God's plan of salvation for mankind could not be accomplished.

To Jesus, the will of the Father settled every question. He came to earth to do the Father's work, not His own—even though it meant He had to suffer greatly. From beginning to end, His life here on earth was one of total self-sacrifice.

In the midst of your hurts, are you yielding and praying that God will have His way? May Jesus' example serve as an encouragement to you!

A Compassion That Never Changes

Jesus Christ is the same yesterday, today, and forever.

HEBREWS 13:8

Can you imagine a Jesus who never weeps in compassion for the lost and hurting? A Jesus who refuses to forgive Peter for denying Him? A Jesus who gives up on the disciples because they were of little faith?

Can you imagine a Jesus who is never assaulted by Satan and temptation? Who never experiences the heartaches and pains of being misunderstood, rejected, or betrayed? Who, instead of praying to the point of sweating blood shortly before His crucifixion, decides to walk away because the pain just isn't worth it? Who, while on the cross, tells the thief, "Sorry, but it's too late for Me to save you. You've already had your chance"?

In Jesus we find the total opposite. He abounds with love, mercy, and compassion. He is incredibly patient and longsuffering. He is ready to forgive, knows our every need, and will never desert us.

The Jesus we see in the Bible, who lavished care upon the afflicted of yesterday, is the same Jesus who cares for our hurts today.

In Anticipation of Glory

Through many dangers, toils, and snares,
I have already come;
'Tis grace hath brought me safe thus far,
And grace will lead me home.

When we've been there ten thousand years,
Bright shining as the sun,
We've no less days to sing God's praise
Than when we first begun.

JOHN NEWTON
"AMAZING GRACE"

The Hope of Heaven

You have a better and an enduring possession for yourselves in heaven.

HEBREWS 10:34

What treasures do we have on earth that are better than the treasures waiting for us in heaven?

The King James translation of Hebrews 10:34 says we have an "enduring substance" in heaven. All of what we have in this temporary world is but a *shadow* compared to the real and lasting *substance* awaiting us in eternity.

Eventually we will lose everything we have here. By contrast, Peter tells us we have an "inheritance incorruptible and undefiled and that does not fade away, reserved in heaven for you" (1 Peter 1:4).

Here we have uncertainty, there we will have certainty. Here we have troubles, there we will have peace. Here we have sorrow, there we will have joy. *Everything* about heaven is better. The more we consider our future home, the less appealing our present home looks.

When you are in need of comfort, look heavenward. You have much to look forward to!

The Assurance of Victory

In the world you will have tribulation, but be of good cheer; I have overcome the world.

JOHN 16:33

Because we live in a fallen world, we can fully expect tribulation. It is the norm, not the exception. We are travelers in the wilderness, in a land ruled by an enemy who is opposed to God and all who belong to Him. Danger lurks all around, inviting us to stumble and be filled with fear.

Even then, our Lord exhorts us to "be of good cheer." He knows our tendency to buckle under the weight of our circumstances. And He urges us to not be discouraged. "But He doesn't know how greatly I suffer," we may say. Yet He does know, for when He walked upon this earth, His suffering was far greater. And He went on to win the battle—over sin, over Satan, over death.

"I have overcome the world," He tells us. He has already conquered all that we struggle against. No matter what the outcome of our trials here on earth, no matter how difficult a road we must walk, ultimately, we will overcome the world, too.

Be of good cheer, for in Christ, we are conquerors!

Not Worthy of Comparison

I consider that the sufferings of this present time are not worthy to be compared with the glory which shall be revealed in us.

ROMANS 8:18

The apostle Paul drank deeply from the cup of suffering. If anyone had reason to become discouraged and defeated, he did. What helped him to keep running strong in the face of overwhelming difficulties?

He knew the sufferings of this world are brief. Time is fleeting. It passes by quickly. Life's trials are limited to "this present time" and will not follow us into eternity.

He knew the glories of heaven are eternal. Someday we will enjoy bodies that experience no pain or sorrow. We will no longer struggle with problems of any kind. Instead, we will be perfect and immortal…forever.

Paul knew that afflictions are temporary, and glory is permanent. He said the difference between the two is so vast they are "not worthy to be compared." Our many years of suffering here on earth will vanish into nothingness within our first minute in eternity. What a glorious hope we have before us!

A Glorious Future

Your sorrow will be turned into joy.

JOHN 16:20

Little did Jesus' disciples know just how intense their sorrow would be within the next few hours. The Teacher whom they loved dearly would be torn away from them and crucified upon a cross. In great fear they would scatter and hide, totally at a loss over what to do next. Life as they knew it would come to a sudden and devastating halt.

Yet Jesus promised them their sorrow would be turned to joy. Though the tribulation that lay ahead was great, the victory that would follow would be even greater. The sorrow they endured for a few days would be well worthwhile because it meant an eternity of rejoicing.

Though Christ spoke these words in relation to His death and resurrection, the joy He promised is for all believers for all time. There is coming a day when we will no longer suffer, and our fallen, mortal bodies will become risen, immortal bodies. In that day, all the tragic results of man's fall into sin will forever cease and be replaced by all the benefits of Christ's victory over the grave. When that day comes, our sorrow will indeed be turned into joy!

Appointed to Suffering...
and Blessing

No one should be shaken by these afflictions; for
you yourselves know that we are appointed to this.

1 THESSALONIANS 3:3

Afflictions are unsettling. They make us realize just how little control we have over our lives and circumstances. They come when we don't expect them, and their unpredictable nature is what makes us fearful when they strike.

But the apostle Paul says we shouldn't be shaken by afflictions because "we are appointed to this." Because we live in a fallen world we should expect to suffer, and God, in His sovereign wisdom, allows us to suffer.

While it's hard to fathom how God can use affliction for our benefit, He does. The good news is that our appointment with affliction is temporary. As Christians, we have also been appointed to blessing—for all eternity! We have the promise of everlasting life, peace, and joy, which can't be taken from us. In Romans 8:30, Paul wrote that those whom God justified, "these He also glorified." He wrote about our future glorification in the past tense—as if it had already happened. That is how confident we can be about the blessings of heaven!

The View from Mount Eternity

God will wipe away every tear from their eyes;
there shall be no more death, nor sorrow, nor
crying. There shall be no more pain, for the former
things have passed away. Then He who sat on the
throne said, "Behold, I make all things new."

REVELATION 21:4-5

Someday we will stand with God at the top of Mount Eternity and look back upon the landscape below and see, for the first time, a clear panorama of this long journey called life. We will see the sharp precipices, the steep switchbacks, the treacherous rockslides that challenged us. We will also see the spacious green meadows, the quiet lakes, and the shade-filled pastures where God gave us rest and renewed our strength.

On the way up the mountain, we could only see the trail in bits and pieces. Frequently our vision was blocked by canyon walls, nearby hills, and tall trees, making it difficult to get our bearings or know whether we were even making progress. Some stretches of the trail were so dark we had only enough light for the next step. Other times we faltered momentarily, seduced by temptations along the wayside. Time and again we cried out to God for help.

And more times than we could count, we realized that if it weren't for our all-sufficient and all-knowing Guide, we would have been hopelessly lost.

When God grasps our hand and pulls us upward for that final step onto the peak of Mount Eternity, at last everything will become clear. We will see how He used all our other steps along the way to build us up so we could persevere as the trail became increasingly difficult. We will finally understand the purpose of every affliction, and how it is that "all things work together for good to those who love God" (Romans 8:28). We will see how God lovingly refined and perfected us, making us more and more a display of His goodness, wisdom, and grace.

As we come to realize the magnitude of God's beautifying work in our lives, we will find ourselves deeply humbled over all the times we doubted and questioned Him. We will bow down before Him, our hearts overflowing with gratitude and praise. We will rejoice like never before because our suffering has finally come to an end. There will be no more tears, no more sorrow, no more pain, no more death…for they will all have passed away.

Night will have ended, and morning will have come. A new day will have dawned, and eternity will have begun.

Notes

1. The inspiration for this devotion came from a J. Vernon McGee sermon that appears on pages 25-53 of his book *On Comfort: Words of Hope for the Hurting* (Nashville: Thomas Nelson, 1994).

2. John Trapp, as cited in C.H. Spurgeon, *The Treasury of David*, vol. 2 (Peabody, MA: Hendrickson Publishers, n.d.), p. 55.

3. James W. Alexander, *Consolation* (New York: Charles Scribner, 1852), p. 217.

4. John Dickie, *Unsearchable Riches* (Kilmarnock, Scotland: John Ritchie, n.d.), p. 40.

5. This devotion appears in my book *One-Minute Promises* (Eugene, OR: Harvest House Publishers, 2006), p. 90.

6. This is a condensed version of the three illustrations, using mostly C.H. Spurgeon's own words, taken from a sermon he preached at the Metropolitan Tabernacle in London on April 2, 1876.

7. "How Firm a Foundation," authorship unknown. This hymn first appeared in John Rippon's *Selection of Hymns*, 1787.

8. Thomas Brooks, as cited by Benjamin Orme, *Treasure-Book of Consolation* (New York: Dodd, Mead & Company, n.d.), p. 28.